Rambling
Through Lanes

Rambling Through Lanes

Ranjit Kumar Sinha

PARTRIDGE

A Penguin Random House Company

To order additional copies of this book, contact
Partridge India
000 800 10062 62
orders.india@partridgepublishing.com

www.partridgepublishing.com/india

SPONSORED BY:
DR SHIRSHENDU SINHA, M.D.
DR SUTAPA SINHA BHATTACHARYYA, Ph. D.
NANDITA SINHA, M.A.

AUTHOR'S ADDRESS:
RANJIT KUMAR SINHA
FU 22 BANKIM SARANI, SOUTH
MATH, JYANGRA
KOLKATA, PIN: 700 059,
WEST BENGAL
INDIA
MOBILE: 91 92306303 88
LAND LINE: 91 033 2570 6858
EMAIL: biophysics66@yahoo.in

Dedicated To the memory of
My Late Parents & In Law Parents
My Late Elder Brothers
(Asit Braran Sinha and Ajit Baran Sinha)

Preface

I publish here my poems for a simple reason that I wrote poems and I should leave them now as the property of the poetry loving community. My wish is fulfilled. My thoughts will remain in my poems for all times to come.

Most of these poems were written over three years, 2011-2014. I am not a professional poet, nor am I a poetry course educated person. Poetry is my passion, and I have been indulging in writing verse since boyhood of 13, first in my mother tongue, Bengali, and then since the age 21, in English too.

My poems issued mostly from personal feelings: pain, pleasure, pang, torment, joy, despair, victory, defeat, betrayal, favor, support, cooperation, amity, understanding, compromise, disbelief, maladjustment, pride and vanity. All veered around my love and respect for humanity. Questions of why, how, what, where on poems could not be answered. 'Cause me too had no control on my passion and feelings, except for social obligations as a conscious person. The readers may explain in their own ways now and decades after. As a scientist I appreciate that a published document has some research value to the posterity, besides becoming enjoyably readable to present readers.

Of late, when I am 70 plus the thoughts of an aged retiree are visiting my composition canvas with their specific hues and textures. I have taken up the brushes to paint out in my own way.

Nature - man interrelations, rather than man to man interactions, are getting prominence to me. Nature excluding man in my social existence does not mean anything significant so much, man inclusive of nature all around has been importantly appreciated and understood by me; the concern was human welfare.

Politics is pervading social and natural environments. Political inflictions and afflictions, inhuman Terrorist Violence, widespread corruption, consumerism, extreme professionalism, globalization of business influenced all categories of writers. Women as half of the sky, environmental concerns, frank opinion against sex discrimination and sexual exploitation, life styles, fast urbanization in developing Asian countries are attracting attention and getting focus for a better world. The poets cannot stand aside. In my poems love and nature got more focus, depression and frustration often overwhelmed. However, it is my malady; my poems would reveal that LOVE is the only remedy I have self prescribed.

My expectation is that Indian poetry readers particularly those living across the world and the readers of all countries, would, on leisure, pick up the publication. Their reactions are welcomed. Mistakes, errors, poet's liberty on twisting language to match poetic need are mine; I beg to be excused for such lapses.

I am thankful to Sri (Dr) Susanta Kumar Patra, HOD, Physiology Department, Surendranath College, Kolkata for his help and encouragement.

My daughter, Dr. Sutapa Sinha Bhattacharyya and my son, Dr. Shirshendu Sinha took active interest all through to publish, assuring me sponsorship. My son virtually forced. They deserve my thanks. Sri Kaushik Bhattacharya, my son in law, deserves a special mention for his silent support. My grandchild Megha (Aiswarya), was the source of inspiration. While writing in potry.com I got so many poet friends all over the world, who reviewed, appreciated, suggested corrections on my poems. I am grateful to all of them.

I was at my wit's end as I had to select about 100 plus poems out of about 900 poems written in English. Who could rescue? Everybody was of the opinion that I would be the best judge. The task was not at all easy for a creator to keep aside some and select others. My wife gave me very practical suggestions. I am thankful to her.

AMIDST ALL PERTURBATIONS IN LIFE AND OUT SIDE MY INNER ME IS CALM AS I GET A CONSTANT COMPANY OF SONGS OF RABINDRA NATH TAGORE. THAT HELPED ME COMPOSE.

Mr. Sudip Ghosh Chowdhury did computer work patiently, overlooking my computer literacy deficiency with his grace and affection.

In fine, apart from poem selection I owe immense gratitude to my beloved wife, Nandita, for sharing my family burden on her shoulders during the course of preparation of the manuscript.

I leave it to readers for ANYTHING to offer that my poems deserve.

Namaste

RANJIT KUMAR SINHA.

EMAIL: biophysics66@yahoo.in
91-9230630388
Fu 22 Bankim Sarani, South Math
Kolkata 700059, West Bengal, India

Contents

1. Rambling Through Lanes

Rambling through lanes of life,
Meandering through nature,
What I so long derived
Is simply LOVE,
a mixture of pang and pleasure.
Love did impart elation,
did bring sometimes tears.
Lanes visited were sometimes lit up,
some times were pitch darker.

But there were no dead ends;
movement was smoother.

My flows, in and out, were made soother
by lives around and by verdant nature.
Rambling through life and nature
What I derived is LOVE,
a harmonious mixing of pang and pleasure.

2. First Love Teacher

See a Mother;
she is the first love teacher.
How she behaves and reacts to her child
is the primary love lesson in all times to abide.

God was the MENTOR,
Nature was the associate,
On love and care teachings
of all mothers of all times.
I am sure,
My mother was a good mentee.
That is why she was superior
to her mentor,
as a love and care provider.

3. Visibility

Heart is clouded,
Visibility is poor.
Nothing is in the canvas beyond self.

A strong wind is awaited.
Let clouds drop as rains,
or, be driven away.

Which way is better?

Rain drops on grass are like pearls -
I prefer.
Driven away clouds leave vacuum -
I fear.

Pit-pat sounds all night,
or, vacuum musing in silence utter?

Clouded heart ponders,
Undecided mind swings.

And as long as visibility is poor
Heart would live closed door.

4. Love Is The Basic

Love is the basic
for science, arts and commerce.
There are a few search lights,
but vast darkened zones,
a few callers for illumination
and
many liking to live in dark
on commodity satisfaction.

Commodity is their motivation,
consumption is their civilization.

Civilization pivots on industrialization,
industrialization is extraction,
extraction uncontrolled is pollution,
pollution begets destruction.

Some say,
destruction inspires creation.
Creations use
a heart -brain combination,
in each step
love for life governs motivation.

5. Love The Only Investment I Go For

Labor, money, capital,
share, mutual fund, business
the whole consumer and commercial indices
are prone to bankruptcy.
But not love insurance, investment policies.
If you have any profit ambition
use 'love' as capital exploitation.
The entire human business
Is in profound distress
for imbalance in investments
On love and care share markets.

Use humanity in this venture
as the central thematic force.
All incarnations stood for love business;
their words through ages
constitute your MBA course.

Heart to heart sales, taking clues from them,
when roll smooth in human market,
all is Profit.
All is yours.

6. Generic

Generic information is a reality.
Given name is a personal identity
amidst thousand copies.
You are entitled to a quote
that you belong to a specific trait and quality.

Nature likes subtle variations.
Man is still finer artificially.
Nature self regulates its qualification;
Man is unruly to deregulate imposition.
Rights are other name of freedom from organization.
Nature has its own inviolable ethics,
And so needs no institution.
Man is ever political
since its genre started;
and needed logistics
for its follies to be aborted.
Social man is a multiplex product.
Environment does regularly
Modify his generic conduct.
We, the mundane men,
Love the fame in a brand.

7. Selfish Living

I continue to live and thrive
despite fellow men were sacrificed
by political knives.
The killed are in the headlines;
the killers are more so, roaming fine.

The media have right to relish;
they twist and turn as they wish.
The police, under power, seem foolish.

If the throne is visible round the corner
the crown cherisher does not anything care.
'Give me blood', the kingdom dreamer clamors,
'I will give you ransom share'.

The most sought after are then the law breakers.
'Do what you like' my money and power will be your savor.

The civil society and the Press are divided
under the cover of dethroning the bad rulers.
Killing they support, they act as blood washers.

Guns and gun powder come across the border.

Politics we cannot do away with.
Can we not minimize politics pollution?
Should we not keep the earth cleaner
for our budding citizens who are dearer
than anything whatsoever?

Selfish poet, you scare.
Who will feed you?
Go to jail.
Feeding is at no cost there.
Forget not,
your pen is ever mightier.

8. Indian Summer

In India it is midsummer.
The Sun is a merciless heat sprayer.
Air is full of moisture.
Clouds are sky frequenters.
But, roaring they are without pouring.
Are living closed door the old, morning walkers.

The sun melts body mightier,
with moisture and fire.
He is the worst sweat producer.
We need a chain of commercial scavengers.

Sell well in the market the body powders.
Mothers are feeding the playing children
glucose, saline water.
The poet is the worst sufferer.
Somehow he finds an AC-cooled corner,
and works lazily with his computer.

Poems are few and far between.
Words have gone to hilly resorts.
Verses too, like Sun burn fearing damsels,
are hiding their skin in cool comfort.

Oh! Summer,
Leave us quicker.
Instead, give us low pressure.
Incessant rains we will venture.
Summer! Leave us, leave us, summer.

Summer did pay heed to the prayer,
At once sent clouds with a storm carrier
To incessantly shower heavier.
At many places came huge deluge.
Yet on any lame excuse
We could not say,
'Stop low pressure'.
Summer and Rains tied together.
We played as idiot onlookers.

9. Scary Tale

Half of the sky is above me,
half below,
the sea is spinning fast,
half of the mountains hang piteously,
still I do not scream, do not cry.
How am I?

Seas are suspending,
Lakes too,
Trees are suspending,
And he, she, you.
They say,
It is for love towards the power of Centre.
Alas! I live in a periphery town.
If I fly off some day centrifugally to nothingness
My LORD,
Would you spare!

10. Closed And Open

You were all open to me.
Clothes heaped on the floor.
Closed was the door.
Through a half opened window
Spring breeze did me implore,
'It is the right time,
Closed eyes you lay on the floor.'
I obliged.

You asked me,
'what did you see'.

My closed eye balls pierced through eye lids.
I said,
'I saw your heart,
I saw your soul,
what you had so far hid'.

You boxed my ears and said, 'a clever kid'.

Then my turn was to bare.
Your turn was to stare.
You did not close your eyes.
Closing eyes for a woman was not wise.

I asked, 'what did you see?'
You said, with mute smile,
'my eyes are dazzled.
I could see only through my mind gate.
Your body was all strength to elate.
It was agile and straight, all good and great'.

With this pleasing semi truth
I could not be that brute.

Next morning when we woke up fully clad
Sunshine greeted us placid and glad.

11. The Humanity Weeps

The barrel of the gun rotates;
today the bullets are on their chest,
you are glad.
Humanity weeps.
Political barrels change hands and hue.
That tomorrow creeps stealing;
The barrel rotates
One hundred and eighty degrees.
And bullets land on your chest.
Humanity weeps again.
Politics, left or right, under the sleeve laugh.
We, the fool, shout and cry for a day.
Comes in abundance
for the killed political tears and bluff.

12. Sweet Lies

Sweet is your face,
attractive are your legs,
enticing are all pieces in between,
you are a cupid queen.
The whole world knows,
friends and foes,
that you are off and on mine.
I am all praise
not only for your face
but too for your base.
Of late, I make out
What are those
very special in you
that I love most?
Of late I realize
it is your plenty lies
that you so easily pour
day and night,
at moments right.
This is your ingrained vice.

I swear, I will shut your mouth
if you ever tell me a single truth.
Sweet are lies
when told in whisper
to invigorate my dampened temper.

13. River

When a man and a woman
had swum across a river hand in hand
they knew not what waited in the other bank.
Both of them were turned into 'He and She' wolves.
They loved and fought the whole day full.
When they came back
they parented a twin: love and hate,
to rear them through life's varied lasting gates.

14. Updates

Updating has been the way of life,
Update, or Perish,
Updated you flourish.

Backdated wisdom will not to sell,
even on 'buy one get two' retail.
The backdated are trash,
they are bound to crash.

The history repeats, some say.
Is modern science an update, in any way?
Fairy tale angels' wings
are far more versatile than airship engines!

Are we repeating and updating
what we have been imagining?
Do we imagine and contrive
from our prehistoric settings!

When we fight and destroy
Do we do that to update our golden past?
Do, we update our greed and lust?

Updating is a necessity to compete and survive,
the backdated fall back
in every field of life.

15. From An Alien Land

Now and then mentally I visit the house
where my mom lapped me,
my sisters, out of affection, slapped me,
on my victory my friends clapped me.

Those days in country home
brings back memory in red hues
as in the spring there
bloom galore the Palash flowers. (a beautiful red
color flower representing advent of spring)

Those days bring back
the scorching summer,
down pouring rains
and mild winter.

The land was rough and dry,
water was scanty, dust plenty,
people were simple and rustic.
Love was in abundance;
they emoted often but at the same breath
they were rural like realistic.

There the shadows of a huge banyan tree
was comfortably cool,
there the crystal clear natural water
filled the swimming and fishing pools.

There grass was green,
dew drops were like pearls,
birds did sing,
with them, sang
the cow grazing girls.

Career quest took me away
to a far off alien land,
my parents are in heaven;
the village mother would ever remain alive
in my fond reminiscence.

16. Yellow Leaves

Yellow leaves dropped,
Green buds crawled in.
I ever walked in between.

I too would drop.
And then be picked up
to be buried or burnt.
Every living entity
has its turn.

Before I depart
I would dig earth,
I would sow seeds,
water plants,
trim branches,
fence flowers.

And then collect fruits.

What I gather
I would share
with the third world sufferers
who put hard labor.
But for food
At other's face they stare.

17. Rivulet

A simple, uneducated girl in misery
when she got a recovery
out of her day to day peril
she sat knelt down.
And staring at my face
she clearly muttered,
'you are my God'.

'Yes!' I said, 'It is God
who rescues and puts in order,
there is no wonder'.
I am a simple abider.
She continued,
'But you are no less any way.
To my dirty life you offered clear water.
I now bathe here naked without fear.
Cool comfort, as you are,
I long cherished and desired a rescuer
from the time I had left my last male partner.
You taught me:
'Love making is not a fun.
Be prudent coin wise by preserving,
In course of your day to day contact,
What you collect and earn'.
You are well set.
That is what from me God wants.

18. God Concept

GOD created man
Or, Man created God.
I am in a permanent dilemma.
Man is imagination endowed animal;
Anything he can do by imaginative manipulation.
That is why, whatever man has done
I doubt the basic meaning and sense.
About God I am lost in the labyrinth
of various concepts and realizations.
I stay away from gods but not from their teachings on peace
and prosperity of human. Their sayings over ages and times
Reverberate in my mind.
As I sum up and surmise
I get the clues; from different hues
I combine as does the nature.
I get from the combination
'WHITE' an all engulfing beauty.
That is I my GOD, with hundred percent certainty.

19. Monotony

Monotony is in every beauty.
It is an extreme cut off situation.
Be it in hills, lakes, seas and falls.
After a few days you need call
for shift in attention and position.
You are hungry to get a fresh companion.
On any fancy price
Soul does not want to submit to monotony;
You ought to
give him a changing address,
and sweet alternative company.
Tulip too is eye teasing in monotony.

20. Oh, My Poems!

Oh, my poems!
Can you not become
so great, good, and a grace
that lifting up my face
I can call my GOD to say,
'you have given sound,
that is why the birds sing,
and the fountains giggle;
You have given sonorous alphabets,
that is why spoken words
are so pleasing, soothing and sweet.
And you have enabled us to build up language
with such a grace
that through poems what we express
enter all hearts, and ease stress.

Oh, my poems!
Do frequently alight
on this soiled earth
from your heaven home,
just like winged angels!

Let all readers marvel
And rejoice
with the sweetest poetic choice.
I, then as a poet, would elate and pride,
Would like to take a chariot ride
with my new, snob bride.

21. Internet Out Of Order

When my internet was out of order
my poetic words did get rest for a while.
But my life!

It was made to go to exile,
Or, to an I.C.U, to recover.

Hey, internet brother!
Do not leave me.
I have no alternative caretaker.

Poems and poetic words!
Do they feel too much abused,
Or, physically tortured?
Do they require holidays
As we do in extreme summer?

I assure,
Hence forward
I shall allow them off days regular
so that they can relax and pamper.

My internet comrade,
without your constant company,
I am deaf, dumb, blind and
an absolute cipher.

22. Exiled

Exiled ever,
my mind sets sail on an unknown journey.
No body, except hunting will, need accompany.
The inner me says,' here no one wants me'.
The outer me supports the plea.
And both together row for an undiscovered sea,
climb the mountains to find hiding dens,
scan the forests for settling with alien friends.
My two me's look, unashamed,
at the beautiful unvisited damsel eyes.
Both of them are unequivocal
on questions of virtue and vice.

As exiled, no familiar faces do ask them,
'who are you and what for here'.
Unperturbed and undeterred they roam,
and sing in praise of the blissful exile.
Two me's are happy.
I am in peace for a while.

23. Sex In Wilderness

When sex seeks to overpower
Love raises its head high.
Body is then perplexed,
In wilderness should it cry!
Sex with love
And love soaked in sex,
Does make life evenly ply?
Wisdom should comply.
Beauty, Love, Sex and Wisdom combined when DRAUPADI*
caught hands of five husbands:
the whole MAHABHARATA learnt the truth:
Family obligations to keep unified
were above personal amorous desires.

Sex behaved.
Lust too. Love behaved.
Society was saved
From sex related wilderness.

---

* **Draupadi**, the most beautiful princess whom ARJUNA won for marriage in a sayambar competition, had to marry five brothers of Arjuna (including Arjuna) under the dictate of Kunti, the mother of those five brothers. It was indeed a necessity for Kunti to keep the sons united.

24. Obedient Nature

How seconds, minutes, hours,
Packaged in a day, are
Obedient to NATURE,
any way.
GOD obedient is my lovely nature,
Nature does obey
the rotational rule of system solar,
as per God's order,
in perfect continuity
with utmost sincerity!

I had thought,
they could be a bit disobedient,
Instead of gliding evenly in the solar home
they could become, at times, turbulent.

Alas!
Nature never uses judgment.
Whereas since I learned tact
I am wisdom arrogant,
challenging and questioning the rules
those come from top administration.

Nature,
Father of our fathers
and mother of all mothers!
Excuse me;
In false human vanity
We could not estimate
why obedience
Is your pride, prestige and gravity.
Why you need work
with absolute integrity.
Why storms, typhoons, deluges, earth quakes
are to obey your divine laws.
Some of your set duties
we call cruel as they go against human interest,
as if, nature is meant for man only
others you may reject!

25. No Calling Back

The spring just bids good bye
leaving behind for us
fragrant flowers and verdant foliages.

It was a liberal departure.
Rather, we were ashamed
of not being able to offer
the highest price of our heart
to that wonderful wanderer.

Don't call him back.
She has to blossom flowers
in all backyards
of the Western gardeners.
She has to heed to their prayers.

I would rather implore,
'Do not delay your arrival next year'.

The truth is:
The spring will proudly make an advent
as soon as there is 'goodbye'
of the harsh Winter.

Came the long waited summer
at MINNESOTA, ROCHESTER.
My sweet Grand Daughter is ready
to sow seeds and plant saplings of flowers.
Sitting in India I will rejoice with the pictures
sent by her through satellite brother.

26. Drizzling Morning

Beautifully drizzling morning!
The sweetly singing sky!
Indoor are staying morning walkers.
None would brave a drenching.
I heaved a huge sigh.

After this chiming drizzling,
at our doors
autumn would be knocking.
Rain drops on grass blades
will look as pearls shinning.

My love girl would be picking
grass kissing jasmines.
Her pet bird would love chirping
a melody matching the drizzling.
In joy every nook and corner
would be bee like buzzing.
It is drizzling.

The morning Sun is imploring;
'Why the crazy clouds are yet weeping'.
All quarters are beaming.
The poet is relaxing.
No more poems are to walk in.
It is their French leave.
They would come again
Tomorrow morning.
Everybody knows,
behind the weeping clouds
the graceful Sun is smiling.

27. Give Me

Give me
a green sky,
a blue meadow,
a milky river,
an orange mountain,
a golden desert,
a violet beach.
Bring back
the receding horizon
to my reach.

Help me out
from traditional agony
of ancient colored company.
I would go for a fresh
honey moon destination
as soon as my prayer
gets your clearance.
Actually, the demands are not mine,
they are of my disobedient heart.
The heart says, 'try once with the sky green'.
'It is more pleasing
than the traditional blue', you will find.
'Do not say nonsense'
by your physics learning.
With the sky green
You would too proudly grin.

28. Combination Concert

When rhymes come fluently in your pen
and rhythms do accompany,
poems become just like falls,

The poet walks almost still,
not to break the murmurs of dry leaves.
Is added to that murmuring
a rivulet's pebble dancing.
GOD is obliviously playing HIS
concert with rapt attention.
The whole world listens to
nature's rhyme rhythm combination.

29. Golden Cage Bird

My golden cage lively bird!
I am blind to your love.
My eyes failed to see you had wings,
you had your desire to fly out and in,
you had your mind and brain to sing.

Had I known before
I could have fed you opium more,
made you sleepy and cool,
made you a permanently obedient, fool.
What is the worth of putting you in a chain of gold
if you are clever and so bold,
if you have longing to scan the sky,
without my permission if out you fly?

Learn to love your golden cage,
feed on opium and chosen grains.
I will put around your neck
A 22 carat, hall marked,
heavier chain.
My wife also loves chains.
Is she a gold loving bird
loaded with longings and desires?
She scares freedom.
Let her be cage debarred.

30. Sharing

Sharing a poem with the poet community
Is to share your philosophy on life,
your concept on global village,
your longing for universal access,
your concern on extraction menace,
your soul searching interrogations
on pollution and corruption,
your anxiety on communal conflicts,
your voice against first world deceits,
your literary depictions and designs
to speak out your heart through poetic lines.

And to let everybody know, you are in oneness
with one and all in this planet and beyond.
You are, for peace and prospect, a real champion.

Your heart to heart communication
enables you to eliminate hate and indignation.

As you progress connecting and sharing poetry
you enjoy a unique position in the global society.
In overall aspects of harmony and integrity
you are then an individual with universal fraternity.

31. My Love My God

She asked in whispering tone
'Do you love me, only me?'
I said, 'yes,' I said, 'no'.
Then, why here, you may go.
I said, I am balancing my 'yes' and 'no'
'Cause in "yes",
You are my respect,
my awe, my wonder;
you are just as good as nature.

And in "no",
We hate, scream, and disbelieve
each other,
just as two long time foes.
'Love' is yes, 'Hate' is no.

Whom would you worship?
You asked.
'Why?
'My love'.
I flashed.
'What love?'
Love I will,
In general,
'Nature',
In particular,
'your character and features.'

You insisted,
'What is your service to God?'
I persisted,
'My God is not a temple dweller.
But to anywhere everywhere
He has Himself scattered.
My service to God is my service to nature'.

'Does it include man'?
Does it include criminals and despots '?
'Yes, of course.
Services are accordingly different.
But services are loaded in reverence'.

What and how do you pray to your God?
I pray,
'Oh! God,

Enable me to protect and preserve.
Enable me to love and care.
Enable me to ignore hatred and malice,
I will do then undaunted carry on my service.
My woman, my love,
You are indeed to me
special part of nature.

32. Diametrically Opposite

Women and men
Bed they share,
Wed they glad,
But they never stay together
as their mental kingdoms
are located
in two diametrically
opposite hemispheres.

Everybody knows.
The truth nobody utters.
'cause by a magician's wish
Woman and man
Are bed sharers.

33. A Small Fry

Better, best, worse, worst
In grammar happily lie.
Where a small fry,
as me, would out fly?
Tell me, 'is it to the empty sky?'

Throughout my early life I was shy
to make a steady start, and
to ask if I leave behind the nest for you
What, in lieu, I would come by.
You know, for my lack of courage,
I was identified in your passionate world
as a small fry.
But then I made a desperate fly
into the poetic sky.

From a dust tarnished walk
My fly did help me revive
my shine and stripe.
Amidst the poet community
Now I am proudly alive.

Now I can cry;
'I am not a small fry.
Poems brought back the trust
that I should strive to last.
Flying or Swimming I should reach
the infinite rhyme beach.
In the ever deep blue of words
A poet flyer is not a small fry.
MY LOVE GIRL!
A few poetic lines
why can't you try?

34. Not The Same

Birth day comes cycling once in a year.
Each time it differs.

Each time you advance,
you gradually ripen,
green to mature, burnt brick color.

Your birth days do whisper,
'you transform
from daughter to bride, to wife, to mother.
You were all along loved and cared.
Now it is your turn to return and spare.'

Birthdays come year after year
following the solar calendar.
Each year
life changes in texture, grain and color.

Social functions are admittedly a great fun;
more you enter into their vortex,
worse you are grilled and churned.

35. Dawn

At Dawn
Streets and areas common
are relatively free from human pollution.

Most people sleep,
or, some about to get up and peep.
The Sun prepares
in the backdrop, for a fight, to equip.
I just leave the bed
to shake off lassitude's grip.

A cool, soothing breeze
lazily entered from the hill cliff
to say an undue 'HEY, HALLO,
Open your door and open the window,
welcome the eastern glow,
will soon begin the day's show,
soon the morn will intervene,
soon will start the flight of friendly crows'.

Dawn!
You are too transient
like falling jasmines,
or, like vanishing dew pearls
in my backyard garden.

Dawn!
Let the Sun go,
let the moon sleep.
Through my misty window
come again and peep.

Dawn!
Like hope for lost love's return
Come again
through my mental gate
to my spiritual garden.

Life is full of trivial rises and falls,
Life demands dawning of miracles.

36. Looted Liberty

Our liberty is at her/his mercy.
'Our agony is ecstasy,
and ecstasy is agony'
according to his/ her advocacy.
This is a neo democracy:
'I rule, rules my party.
Mine is the sole liberty,
yours is at my mercy.'
'Accept or go to hell'
Is her/his prophecy.

Liberty looting is going on
in two hands
by the charismatic champion.

Fool citizens!
Unlimited is your greed and ambition.

Individual is a non-entity.
Sell your conscience to power party;
Party would give you limited liberty.
To be happy with whatever you get
is your bounden duty.

Set your priorities of how to live proper,
Get it endorsed by the party in power,
Live the life as they desire.

Individual is a misnomer.
Valueless is your inborn and earned caliber.
Are you a soul searching researcher,
Discover the truth bare:
The political GOD IS GOD PROPER.

History repeats:
As once AJATSATRU* had declared:
and 'SREEMATI, the maid, was a rejecter,
for that her head lost the shoulder.

Looters loot liberty.
Lick the looters boot,
or, they will molest you, uproot.

---

* A Hindu king who banned LORD BUDHHA'S worship from
his Kingdom.

37. Demolished Democracy

Fathers of Indian Constitution
Wake up breaking the burial soil.
Your dream democracy is a spoil.
Leaders demolishing democracy
Are gaining absolute supremacy
on power, politics, money and muscle.
They make the society a jungle
to be lived by cannibal animals.
They loot democratic and human rights
To favor their party and party men
by influencing the lawful administration.
Day by day situation is so grim and grave
Love is replaced by lust,
lust is leading to wide spread rape.
Democracy is raped, humanity is raped.
In a demolished democratic structure
Set systems are not allowed to work.
If leaders do not, Who else would behave.
For god' sake, repair the democracy,
give back human rights.
What else people would want
if living conditions are conducive and bright.

Now the people are powerless onlookers.
They are made to dance like puppets
to save their shelters and shoulders.

Political refugees are rampant in their home land,
Have no asylums, no supporting hands.

The careerist young generation
is fully devoid of moral conscience.
'One man one vote' is not getting due concern
from the voters
who are totally after
their own career.
The country and democracy suffer.
Who cares!

38. Reverse Gear

My dear ancestors!
You had been long in the forest,
Listened to songs and music
of fountains, birds, and to brook's gimmick.
Today, your children like me,
Listen to deafening concerts,
and glorify the home theatre art.

And tomorrow
No ear will hear anything.
Drums will give in.

Because of abuse
God will refuse
In future
to grant us some limbs of use.
Many tomorrows will pass.
Forests will again grow up,
Birds will be again melodious,
Fountains and falls will be sweetly sonorous.
Ears and noses will filter
Sounds and smell harsher.

Our genes will reverse
to make us as we were before.
The new civilization will change the gear
Commercial din and bustle will disappear.

Nature is itself perfection.
She will not tolerate any further
Cunning human manipulation
In the name of scientific inventions.

39. Sutapa* Was Born

(Birth day tribute of an obliged dad)

That was a humid and sultry Sunday.
Last night it rained cats and dogs.
The whole sky was overcast
With ash colored clouds.
And Sutapa
Our dream, our imagination,
Our all cherished aspirations,
Our soulful desire
Was born
fulfilling all our prayer and intention.

We, parents, were close to thirty.
We were immortally thirsty
to drink ambrosia from lips of our child,
our first human exercise,
to pay back debt to our own parents,
a homage and gratitude so nice.

Sutapa was named by her grand Father.
Sutapa* means the lover of the lord SHIVA.

40. Pang And Pleasure

In personal life
my pang is from a biting snake,
my pleasure is words' Michigan Lake.
In the former I am a snake charmer,
In the other I am an apprentice swimmer.
Pang is always the long lived winner.
Pleasure is the transient sweetener.

41. Bird Twittering Morning

At 5 am,
a few small birds started chatting.
What else they could chat about
except on the daily routine.
They spoke about the novel fencing;
They spoke about sharing and chasing.
They discussed how insects they feed on
are gradually modernized and better ducking,
how grasses are scarce,
how mutual and self help,
without political support,
is now-a-days so scarce.

Then they advised their off springs
to stay in door,
make breakfast on the overnight left over.
They promised them good gifts
and a sumptuous treat in the evening later.
He and she then made love on beaks,
and kissed the young on cheeks.

If it clicks, and
Work the risk and tricks,
they would befool the prey,
Have collections fantastic.

Man is apt in befooling act.
From man the birds must have learned the tact.

They then looked for my help all around.
I said, 'I will not let you suffer,
why don't you do politics
to gain a grip on food.
Political power would give you strong ground'.

They smiled and said,
'of course, in the next life
if we were just like you, man.'

42. What A Poem Roamed

What a poem roamed in my sky!
For long it did wave its wings.
For long it did not like to sit on a brink.
For long it encircled the field of corn.
For long it dreamed off ripples of Bengal Ocean.
Then it reached the veil of Niagara Falls.
I gave her a yelling call,
'Come back to my Ganges plain
or, be seated on the Himalaya Mountain.'
My poem did declare:
'To roam in the sky free
is my birth right pleasure'.

43. Mighty Leveler

Cloud after cloud rushes fast,
Covers the sky in no moment;
Storm encourages the gathering.
Where are you now, my friend?

The breach is possible everywhere
when nature is the leveler.
Dykes flash away like sand grains,
rains knows no affliction and pain,
water level raises high to demolish the pride of concrete.
The huts made on banks with trust and confidence
Float like lightest wood sticks.

The current of universal liquid runs insane.
Straw like light- weight was human vain.
Nature, though a beautification master,
at times in demolishing human structures
Has no conscience and knows no pain.

Clouds were totally unaware
that their whim would bring about such a jolt
of leveling all lot
in a single, wanton washing shot.

The poor and the rich
kneel down to beseech,
'Oh, the otherwise beautiful clouds
Stop please, your vagaries'.

44. Cool Inner Bosom

Ripples or waves,
River or sea,
whichever you may be.
I like to float
in a boat or without a boat.
Not even a life jacket
I would take.
If I am drowned
it is your bottom,
cool inner bosom.
I am so fortunate.

45. No Rest

Who will allow rest to waves in the seas?
Who will ask winds to idle away?
Who will stop decay and growth of lea?
Who will cease proliferative process?
Nature has once been started to act
It is a fact, it is a fact.

I, as part of nature,
apart from birth, growth, decay and death,
Do think and muse,
do accept and refuse,
do discard and reuse.

I am a special nature.

I do create and destroy.
I am nature's unruly boy.
No rest knows my supercomputer brain.
Momentarily I go,
but vigorously I come back again.

Melancholia inflicts deep
in me,
Then a poem peeps.

And if the POEM gets a lovely exposure
all my sadness vanishes like vapor.
I am again in mirth.

A poem can take away all anger.
In a humid and hot summer
my poetic words give me a cool bath.
If you are glad
What more you want
in this soiled earth!

46. Veil Be Lifted

Life, let me love you once again,
let your veil be lifted,
your creamed face seen.
Let your beaming smile
be all the more inviting
to forests and fountains
where life is still virgin,
where birds twitter free,
and grasshoppers jump in glee.

Let my mind flow once again
with ripples on lakes.
Let my heart touch the earth
of both the banks like waves that break
Just to be able to kiss and embrace.

My life!
Do, please, make a vigorous restart
so that
all my 'no more please' appeals
Vanish smart.

47. Asleep

When sleep denied, you fail to take rest,
and when all disorderly thoughts share your bed,
when a back calculation makes you a nonentity,
when your world suffers from zero gravity,
You wake up and walk up and down the room
and you lose all sobriety.
Meanwhile the dawn breaks for your nude exposure,
you find the Sun to make a harsh disclosure
that you have been scheduled to leave
so that on your bed
Somebody else could be fast asleep.

48. Cloudy Dawn

When the dawn starts with
low pressure generated clouds
And the whole blue is consumed
promising a heavy downpour
I, being in door, implore
to send someone to explore
why in such a day bereft of sunshine
Our work hunting mind
becomes heavy and unkind,
why the mind asks too many questions
about the importance of existence.

Why activities are fashioned
to suppress the essence of illumination?

I ask, 'why the Sun God
is tolerant of cloudy fraud
on human life'

I get the answer from my inner me:
All creations are silent.
Even for the creation of the Sun
No light was summoned;
darkness alone was the important concern.

What does then darkness mean?
Who will answer:
Mr. Hawkins!

49. Swift And Slim

Poem!
The dearest daughter of literature!
You are slim and sleek,
your eyes are fathomless deep,
you smile as a morning rose,
and you move with the gait of a goose.
You are light,
Just as a pigeon feather,
to lift you to bosom is easier,
easier to keep you on back,
and carry on shoulder.
Be seated, my dear,
on lap
to enjoy all the care
I can offer.
Poem! You are just
a love girl; superb.

It's a pleasure to take you to a bar
for friends to share your mind,
your slim outer cover,
and to muse on your deep inner.

Poet's sweetest darling dear!
Hand in hand
I will move with you
from post to pillar.
Who can me debar!

50. In Den On Throne

She was roaring in a den
inviting the sleeping lion elsewhere to join.
Night is just in.
The Moon climbs just above the tall greens.
Stags are long back home.
Hungry owls ponder to roam
for an innocent prey.
It is the time when the lion should obey.

The lion is to obey.
Who can say
the night would behave jolly, later.
Let him come and join swifter.
And full of fore play!
The royal pair though, often lazy,
is not that much laidback
in love, and on a lovely prey.

In den they are obliging.
They two are aging,
tooth strength diminishing,
they ought to start in time
for a nice finishing.

The queen roars.
An owl backed by hooting.
The fox also supported
by 'huukka huua' off and on.
Midnight bell calls ding dong.

The king came on the bed,
the queen beside.
Everybody else, outside the palace,
wished them a happy union
under the placid, lunatic, love prison.

51. A Kick Back Handsome

You had called me to attend.
So what!
I have not gone,
and never will I go
whatsoever displeasure you may show.
It is a game of go if you are gone.
That time you did not come.
This time I give a kick back handsome.

52. Who Is She

Who is she
to discard me?
Who is she
to hate me!
Who is she to unfasten the knot?
Who is she in her heap of flesh
to make me rot!

I have deciphered her all plot.
I have spied her down to her cot.
Now I would be the man
to decide her lot.

53. Molecular Poem

At heart 'am bold,
outside 'am cold,
my friends say, 'am sold
at a price of gold.

54. The Spot Light

The heroine was majestically
moving to the spot light area,
did a few gestures
and dialogues,
and was then waiting for the hero patiently.
She is a new find.
The hero is an old wine.
A call came.
The hero was absent on excuses lame.

The director yelled, 'call the villain'.
On request the villain intervened.

The heroine was angry and upset
though she presented a look picture perfect.
The villain spoke 'Madam, I am also a new find,
cooperate and be kind
for mutual survival and family upbringing.

Both of them looked confident and cool.
The heroine surpassed herself from all yesterdays.
The villain performed as good as any hero
from a to z by all means and in all ways.
Many clapped and shouted, 'bravo, bravo',
replace the hero by the villain,
teach a fitting lesson to the hero truant.

To that the director called
both to his private chambers
and dispensed with them
from the job then and there.

The hero came next day with his g' friend
she was ushered in as a heroine.
The film flopped.
Director was shacked.
The driven out heroine and villain
came back with redoubled pay packs.

55. Words Broke Silence

Words broke silence
seeing her countenance,
and said,
'I was mute at five
when as a child of four
she was cute galore.
Now at sixteen
her virgin lips apart she grins,
fragrance in her being is full to the brim.
If words were mute at this moment
the poet must not have been forgiven
for describing her majesty
for words' limitations.

56. Tears

Cry was assured from moment of birth.
Tears is an endowment attached to earth.
Tears I inherit,
tears I transfer,
tears is no mean treasure.

I shed tears when I had lost the crown.
I hid tears when I was unduly knocked down.
Hidden tears torment the heart most.
With free flowing tears pang is sealed and closed.

On success, tears are blissful expression on.
Tears are pride when is achieved an ambition.

Tears of weal,
tears of woe, tears of shame
and of shaken faith, belief
all look the same in watery appearance.
Let scientists analyze;
they may find difference
in molecular biology composition.

57. Finite To Die

Anything finite will die down
In its shape and construction
be it earth or be it the Sun.
But the infinite constantly is being woven.
Its loss is beyond detection and imagination.
Selfish thoughts cry,
if we ever die
what will happen!
The infinite laughs and says,
I remain.

58. Heart Is Bigger Than The Universe

God is ever creating this universe never ending,
and He is proud of this whim.
I am amused;
my heart is larger than what God could imagine.
Because, with love in it
Heart is also creating, never ending.

59. Cloud Riding

My mind often rides on back of clouds.
It floats with its companion from east to west.
The vast empty firmament is its cherished home.
The east whispers; soul is above material gains.
The west negates and directs to take pains
Collecting and plundering happiness
from commercial trends.
My mind overlooking from its white cloud seat
Has no guts
either fully to submit to the concept of the east,
Or, to subscribe the practice of the west.

Conflicts continue.
Days glide by.
Riddles stay.

Clouds shake wings to get rid of me.
Where my mind falls
is a saline sea.
Mind muses; it was in search of glee.
The question stands to the moment:
To be or not be!

Conflicts reign.
Commotion interspersed by calmness
is the continual gain.
Rimjhim rimjhim rimjhim
Plays the concert the July rains.

60. Celebration Diamond

'Your love is above and beyond any price'.
You told me in the honey moon night
when the queen of the sky
did glide by
over our heads on a sandy shore.
Waves did sing love lore,
wind did unwind all closed doors,
the Moon light washed our dirty floor.

You got up next morning fresh and vibrant,
asked me, 'where is the celebration diamond'.
I said, 'it was so long with me'.
As you whispered, love was above any price,
I believed.
I was ashamed of the gift,
and threw the diamond into the sea.

61. Wall

Wall is ever.
Ever it is between two of any variety.
Be it person, race, community.
Be it politics, social philosophy.
Be it about care, hug and kiss.
Be it about war and peace.

Wall stands alert
between mind and heart,
between tradition and cult.

Walls vanish
to the blind and the fool.
They say, 'ignorance is cool'.

62. Me - You

Me you, or, reversely, you me
is the root of all agony and ecstasy.
Thousands of poem were written,
millions will be inked down.

As long as this earth
with its nature would flow to infinity
you me or me you will have its continuity.

What is this you me?
It is just two souls among millions
who can isolate out easily,
make flows from and to.
It is just a world
uniquely created
for two communicating hearts.
It is just love, love and nothing else than love.
Have you ever seen GOD!
No.
But you have felt.
It is also only felt and felt and felt.

63. Death

Death does mean many things.
It is just the end of a journey.
It is transferring right and liabilities.
It is just creation of space
for others to fulfill.
It is just being up rooted and thrown
so that others can enjoy the nutrients.
It is just repeating the act
that was enacted many times.

Death does never mean an irreparable loss.
Alive persons and souls have no time
to weigh death's pros and cons.
Customary services are too hypocrisy
to console the dead.
If the dead had any scope
it could protest.

Or, I do not know
how I would behave
when I am no more
in the mortal cage!

My poet said,
'oh, my life, I have loved you
so much with great conviction,
I would love my death
in same measure and proportions'

64. Wisdom

Nature is like that;
its strength is acquired endowments
through millions of years.
Who does educate nature,
who does make it wise,
or, to act foolish?

There is no dictator.
It is just customary
to act, to continue, to conduct.
Nature is its own product.

Man, when outside nature's purview,
is a horrible animal.
Man needs institution, education
values, senses, systems, rules
despite continual development.
Man is ever imperfect and fool.
Wisdom what they call
is totally a game of see-saw,
up I hang, down you claw.

Man created God,
the wisest creation
for all attributions.

Wisdom is that
man is such a lad
of his imaginary God
for his any play or game
whatever consequences descend
he is only 'sorry' but seldom sad.

65. Oh, Miss

United we live,
united we grieve,
united we climb
all the cliffs.
If we ever slip
we will do united,
this was our promise.
Why do you then
refuse the kiss?
Forgotten are the chapters
We united read
How to traverse the rough road,
how to undone agenda accomplish.

66. Mistake Bricks

My castle wherein I am safe
is built on mistake bricks,
lies all over act as cement;
self deceits are ornamental to inside decorations.
I feel, I have done wrongs to my foundation.

This negative thinking
has engulfed me,
has shaken vigorously my existence;
my gait lacks ambition,
and my word loaded speech is a juxtaposition
of undigested learning and vain education.

Those who are apt to commit mistakes,
mistakes do not leave their pampered company.
They, though, are briefly ecstatic
but in the end
they are victim to endless agony
throughout a rough and tough journey.

67. Promises Are Made To Break

God creates.
But He promises not to preserve creation,
He undoes to do it again.

Man promises to conceal.
Woman gives words
to outwit how she would kill.

Love is short lived in between.
On bed what is clean,
stepping down on gowns on floor
all desires and swearing
are swiftly vanishing.

Smile but don't promise.
God did not send you
to break heart,
Just after one sincere kiss.

68. Happy Birth Day To Meghalbaran

(Name of my Grand Daughter in USA)

Our Meghalbaran
is just like a flower of Eden Garden.
She sings like an angel of heaven.
She smiles like the soothing moon shine.
Is loaded with piety, beauty, humility
her golden mind.
She enchants everybody
where ever she stays.
She is the Aishwarya (treasure)
in all respects and ways.
May the Almighty grant her
the longest ever life span!
It is our sincerest prayer.
Hey, Bhagaban (oh, my lord).

69. Read My Poems

Read my poems to see
how my brain
guides me to think,
how my mind desires me to link
the heart, mind, brain and environment;
how social networks desire me to behave
as a gentleman.

My poems are not only about me
they encompass all I know:
me, my India, my world and time.
All would mix up to reflect,
I was not mere a pawn of fortune.
I played the chess at my best.

70. Deer Plus

I have seen a hare,
so soft and swift,
so cute, so shy, so meek.
I have seen a deer
so beautiful in eyes, legs, skin tan.
So quick.

I have seen you too,
Hare plus deer and something more!
Why different you are, I need explore.
Shy, modest, sincere
whatsoever you are.
You are
my heart enchanter,
my mind enticer and
above all, love arouser.
I stand still when I chance to see the beauty deer.
I was delighted at 7 when I viewed a hare.
At 17, 27, 50 and 70
When I saw you
your eyes and gait
were sweeter than those of a deer.
Oh, my dear!
It was due to a something plus
that resides in heart of a plutonic lover.

71. Sudipta, A Deathless Mortal

Sudipta!
I shall write hundred poems
and thousand songs,
before I die,
on your heavenly fly
to eternal sky.

Sudipta, just at 20 plus
you were pushed to a crash.
You, what a class!
You moved us
with your voice melodious.
With your pen
you outpoured your heart
for the sufferers and the outcast,
for the democratic rights,
against injustice and despotic frights.

You are now ashes in an urn.
Your body was burnt
but your eternal soul
always would roam around
those who needed you most.
You are though out of sight,
you left behind a path so bright.
For every cause you fought
We shall fight.

72. Lust-Love Axis

A man in lust
is in a deep dug well, like a frog,
nothing to hold and climb up.
A man in love is in a crystal clear pond
where he swims, floats, dives free
and gets back to the bank to enjoy glee.

Lust is the end.
Love is the beginning that never ends.
Lust is soul's enemy
Love is a lifelong friend

I have seen a frog to croak in isolation.
I have myself enjoyed pond floatation.
When using lust – love combination
Often lust tries to raise its head,
suppressing love under the feet at the bottom.
Through continuous meditation
You can put down lust
creating for love a congenial situation.
Let lust have its own accommodation.
Let love have its own accommodation.

73. Never Changes

If you tread the tail of a snake
by mistake,
it will straight way curl back and bite,
no matter, you have fed it milk and banana
for years in day and by night.

After all a snake is a snake.

if you beat your dog black and blue,
and throw away the stick,
it will lick your palm,
and in between jaws
give you back the punishing weapon
lest you should require it once again.

After all a dog is a dog.

if you half starve a pet bird
and scold for disturbing your sleep by twittering,
you release it from the cage and say, 'go away,'
it will sit on your window,
part of your bed room,
and call your son's name.

You bring the bird back in shame

After all; a pet bird is a pet bird.

Those who are
grateful are faithful,
by them
love is returned by love.
If you wash a coal piece again and again
Its black character will never change.
If you fire it red hot
White ashes you will probably got.

74. Rimiki Jhimiki Jhim

Rimiki jhimik jhim
Rim jhim rim jhim
All day the rains sing.
Wind is accompanying,
striking lyre strings.

All quarters are vibrating.
Laid back I am listening
Who shouted?
May be clouds,
or, my wife?
'Stop listening,
You, good for nothing'.

I am imploring,
'Rains, Darling,
Stop, please.
It is no longer morning.'

I have to go
for marketing.
She is obstinate.
Singing.
Rimiki jhimiki jhim.

75. Contradiction

Every I is a contradiction
Every you is also not different.
Without contradiction your human machine
cannot run lacking friction.

Contradictions make you stable
in love, hate, lust and trust
Contradictions make you accept
things in life as just or unjust.
My religion is full of contradictions
That is why it survives,
I am the product of that religion
I will strive that its glorious past is revived.

76. Forgive Me

Forgive me.
I know I am tired.
Little might is left in me.
For 70 years I crawled, ran and then walked.
My grandfather was on and on for a century
without fall and injury,
30 years on horseback non- stop.
For him the horse walked and galloped.

For me this is done by my four wheelers.
Still I am tired.
The modern age contributions
of anxiety and tension,
'Hire and fire' business all around
did not allow me to come round.
I am now a bundle of nerves
I do not do, I now sub serve.

Allow me some rest.
Allow me some relaxation.
Allow me some fond breast.
Allow me some smooth inhalation.

Then walk away with me
where ever you choose,
only do not fasten me tight,
lay with me loose.

77. Yet

Yet to go down the line many a miles,
yet to visit many a lanes to see them smile,
yet to reach many a heights of passion,
yet to achieve gettable ambitions,
yet to love who are least loved and cared,
yet to say no to the cheat and swindlers,
yet to win cowardice and timidity,
yet to strive hard to bring amity,
yet to pay off loans of society,
yet to banish the human calamities.
Yet to check out falsehood and deceit.
Yet to ask you,
'Why you left me breaking off at the middle'.
I am yet to solve in my life your riddles.

78. The Chair

It is human nature
to care for the chair.
When on the chair
Poignant is your stature.

You are the leader,
you are the deliverer,
you are the master;
others are to carry out your order.

'Despite haze in your lecture
you are most clear'.—
Are the words of your flatterer.

When you retire and leave the chair
the moment you are a cipher.
The moment you need to pray,
and the next persons on the chair,
to your appeal,
may turn their deaf ears.

The chair matters.

79. There Was A Magician

There was a magician
who touched me with his wand
when I was just a collegian
and thinking to shape me as a Bohemian.

The wand touched my lips first,
then rubbed me all over,
then made me a snake kisser,
and chained me in a hole,
asked me to rock,
asked me to roll.

I only obeyed,
nothing else I could do,
as if, I were the servant,
the wand was my PRAVOO (LORD)

This wand was so kind and affectionate,
yet so rude and merciless
that I had to become a bad boy
what I intended not.
Now I feel
that was my lot
none to change, none to blot!

The wand was deciphered last as
Love for opposite pole,
and I acted simply
my god destined role.

80. Constant

Matter is constant.
Natural balance seems disturbed
out of human abuse and constructions.

But the total effect over of civilizations gone
and civilizations coming up are a constant summation.

We just lament
'cause our stay is too brief,
that brings sorrow and grief,
by rule the sum total is a zero balance.
The infinity laughs under the sleeve
for our extreme lack of prudence.

We kill,
we fell,
we dig,
we block,
we throw, we preserve
for our self satisfaction.
Our activities, added up, are so small!
They are not even ripple like disturbance
to that ocean like CONSTANT.

81. Who Is Beside Me

Who is beside me
when I am tormented,
when I suffer,
when I am depressed,
when I am a loser!

When I elate and exalt,
when I shout out of weal,
when I get the crown
when I am at the peak of zeal.

My soul says,
'your soul mate is your Wisdom;
your friend is your Prudence.
Your strength is your Experience'.

Ponder and muse.
Search your soul.
Many stories you will hear
so far unheard, untold.

82. Money To Any

Money to a woe-man
is pouring water into a bottomless pot.
Nothing is saved
though you have poured a lot.

Extra money with a man
makes him extravagant.
It is just like boiling water
Last drops go into air as vapor.

Money to the prudent
is saved in hives as honey.
It is spent for self
and keeps, to the last, good company.

Money to a miser
makes him so much wiser
that he starves
keeping aside everything for coffer.

Money to me,
Money from me
Is all the more painful
Than a source of pleasure.
'Cause, I do not know
how to spend, spare and share.

83. 14 to 21

I was 21.
And she was 14,
A blackish girl with short height
And with hairs falling down to hip.
To keep them set around the neck
she used a black clip.

She had just experienced
that she was a woman
every month once.
Other than that
She had beside her none.

She, a student,
You, a private tutor.
Thus were spent almost 3 years.

She then 17,
You 24.

Flowers blossomed galore.
Wind was fragrant.
Birds twittered inside.
Oh youth! Thank you;
Thou dist take a good stride.

House was all alone.
Rains intervened.
The town buses stopped plying.
For the tutor
there was no question of home transfer.
Parents were out and the elder brother too.
None could return
There she and you.

Lust surged and overtook.
Flow of hormones gave a rosy look.
She was innocent but wise
You, a novice and fool
You could not keep cool.

She got up and herself cursed.
'Was it a farce?'
She asked.
'It was love plus, plus.'
She blushed.
Thereafter, life was superb.
Bliss, pleasure and cravings
Were shared
without any control and curb.

Then there raised a typhoon
Her doc. brother was fell a victim to an assassin.
She went mad in bereavement.
Her parents too.
The whole world to them lost any meaning.
They were plunged into the sea of mourning.

The sister got hugely revengeful
She was ready to violate all human rules.
For the killer to be killed
She searched all corners far and near.
The police came out to clear the killer.
Those days of revenge taking
She looked like a hungry wolf.
All her grace was gone
All humility forlorn,
All affections off shaken.

She did not calm down.

She was a totally different woman
whom you had never known.
Immense strength
And confidence in her had grown.

'Forget and forgive'
You had told whenever you met.
She was cut and dry and straight
With an emphatic, 'no'
You were scared of that personality show.
Thanks to Almighty!
She had won the battle.
You proved yourself a lover worthless.
In her days of peril
All along you were an almost distant devil.

For this character derailment
GOD has kindly granted you
Very due, lifelong punishment.

Now you stay with a lover,
On a flimsy ground,
Who howls and pounce on you
Like a Royal Bengal Man Eater.

84. Ting Tong

I am like a stringed musical instrument.
Some unknown and yet unseen
Plays on my strings
'Ting, ting, ting
Tong, tong, tong
Ting tong, tong ting ting'.
It just goes so mild
nobody is aware.
I am all the time listening
as I put my ears to my heart,
eyes closed, brain alert.

Ting tong tell me,
I am a part of that infinite,
I can easily unite
my ever immortal soul
with the greatest Whole.
The Whole hides in part
and plays ting tong,
all day long,
all night long,
to time continuum;
my consciousness belongs
to ting tong musical note
that my Almighty father continuously
plays to his beloved nature.

85. Love And Live In Peace

Here white clouds looked aristocratic.
Grey and black clouds were trying to find pleas
to drive out the white clouds to create vacancies.
Lightning, the golden girl, fails to stop the fight.
To wind she submitted wrongs to make right.
Winds gathered strength
and whipped the obstinate.

Quarrels, however, went on.
They wanted poet's intervention.

I said, 'the sky is no body's playing field.
Stay if you like but peacefully, or, get killed.
Roaring and thundering are animal business.
Pouring nature's milk [water] is the kindness
that you are meant to do.
I will this time excuse both of you'.

'Don't weep, dear lightning, any more
I won't allow black clouds to roar.
To accompany your shining smiling
White aristocrats are good for nothing'

I do give you the justice.
Rains are your kind friends,
rains we also like and love.
Live with them in the sky home
with bliss ad peace superb.

86. She Said, Ranjit

When I was 13,
I was traveling by a train,
the first ever tour in railways.
I was thrilled
looking through windows.
The setting sun was
washing us with his golden rays.

In fact, I was going to the divisional town
for a state wise competition.
By that time I had proved myself a scholar,
crossing twice district level hurdle bars.

My eyes were drawn to then two co-travelers,
one girl of 11-12 and one boy of 14.
They, to me, appeared to be sister and brother
Sweet, well dressed with modest manners.

I then took out a book of Treasure,
and though stealthily was looking at the girl
still maintained my composure.

My apparent seriousness pinched the he-man.
The brother hurled a question all on a sudden.
I was in apprehension.
I answered;
then another.
The boy stopped at ten.

Then their father
who was a teacher
braved a few more
all were rightly answered.

The father cried 'a wonder boy'.
My elder brother who was accompanying
Asked me 'a few bombs from your side'
I did oblige.

I said, 'Ten / ten'.
They said, 'What do you mean'.
I said, the first ten you won't be able to answer (I am sure).
The next ten all you would clear.

It happened exactly like that.

They said, 'How come'.
I said, 'Easy.
From your questions I could guess
Your range;
so I went beyond.
But the next ten I gave
within your sphere.
So you cleared.

All the while the girl was looking at my face
with a beam of appreciation and grace,
all along encouraging her brother to sharply chase.

To that soft and beautiful moon
at that dusk
In fact, though a teen ager,
I was feeling the first urge of a lover.

Their parents invited us
to visit them when the test was over.

We could not make it.

After the examination
Some respite I got.
I was taken to some tourist's spots.
Last we came to a beautiful falls (HOODROO)

I went down descending
about 250 steps to touch water.
Exhausted I sat there,
always cherishing a longing
to see once again that face of Shirin (her name).

My amazement!
Giggling of boys and girls of my age
I heard nearing.
To my heart's delight, turning back
I saw
that face.
My heart started throb violently,
And then my breath had dead stopped.

Shirin shouted, 'what a wonder,
that wonder boy is sitting here.'
All her friends cried, 'Is it';
as if, they knew me from head to feet.
Shirin must have told her about our meeting.

There we spent some time exchanging.

That was the last meeting.
Her memory was alive in my mind
covered under dust of time.

When I was 27
and a research scientist,
I was going to attend a seminar.
It was a first class compartment
Only four to share.

I was sitting closed eyes as if in meditation.
There were other three:
One lady, one gentleman and a 3 year son.

It is you, the wonder boy.

Shaking the gentle man the lady said,
'This is he, the wonder boy'.
I opened my eyes amazing.
My heart started violent throbbing.
I calmed down and said,
'What a coincidence, Shirin.
This is really a small globe.
We met again in a railway compartment'.

'How are you, Shirin'?
'Oh fine', she said.
'Meet my husband and my son'.
Husband a handsome man,
the child, cute ever as in Eden.

I took the child within my arms,
Hugged and kissed and kissed;
Praises I showered on GOD
for a meeting like this.

I gave the child a hundred rupee note
to buy a gift.
To the sky him did I lift
and silently whispered to the air:

Could he have been mine!
I asked, 'What is his name, Shirin.'
She said, 'RANJIT'
THE WORLD STOPPED STILL.
Was it my win or defeat!

87. Night Is Still Young

Night is still young,
the sidewalks are busy,
the marts sell brisk.

One teen group sings a melody.

The moon ventures to peep
through dancing and humming leaves,
hips swing, bosoms heave
my wife rehearses a party piece.
I alone sip to a finish.

Life!
would you give back my yester years?
I am no longer hers.
I have read in her eyes
distaste in disguise.
Alone she drives out,
alone she would return.
Of course, her dresses would smell
not as before,
and she won't care
if from heat on my finger tips
I out burnt.

88. Fools' Paradise

Fools' paradise was visited to know
how fools elate there,
how I could fit in.
Oh! it is really an excellent place.
To the fullest extent fools are enjoying.

Don't talk to them about wisdom;
they will kick you off from their kingdom.
They say,
'it is the wise
who deserve a hell.
They are hellish.'
Fools further add:
'we have no agony,
We share only ecstasy and joy,
we have nothing to bother,
none scares us to employ.
Fool's brain is like a super computer.
They don't brood.
Promptly they answer.

Fools love fools
foolishness is their power.
The wise laugh under the sleeve.
Fools don't care.

Fools in their paradise
Laugh at wise men,
saying, you the wise,
to you
Brooding is wise, laughing is foolish.
After death and when alive
we live in a false paradise.

Dust you kiss, sadness is your bliss.
To enjoy the healing power of ignorance
come to our paradise.
Ignorance we practice
Wisdom you relish.

89. *Mid Day*

Mid day in May yet not hot
Rain girls, a few minutes back,
just giggled a lot.
Tree tops are washed of dust and clots,
greens, everywhere greens.
Through clouds just passed a domestic plane.
I am filled to the brim at this moment
with expectations sublime.
Your rainbow umbrella covered your countenance.
I knew, you were coming
from those beautiful longish legs
that had crossed my waist ring
many a times.
Air did unfairly whispered in my ear:
'she is hers, not mine.'
I know you are none
but scorching sun shine,
at present soothing
as cloud girls giggled in between.

90. Open Nature

Before institutions started
nature itself was the greatest institution,
nature was the only teacher.
She was the only school,
she was herself all tools.
She taught through multicolor boards;
green board with leaves
was the largest canvas.
Multi colored butterflies and flowers
were the strongest pupil pullers.
Viewing with open mind, and greenness soothed eyes
slowly help learning and making pupil wise.

And in all conceivable means and ways
nature held out pages after pages
in all earthly entities.
Appreciations come.
Ensue senses of beauty.

Open mind, open heart, open eyes
unplugged ears and naked skin
made human think,
search, discover, invent.
Thus nature made man gradually prudent.

Wise men then said,
'break the walls,
take out the tools,
throw away curriculum,
stop examinations,
tear off certificates,
go back to all open.
Be man, the placid man.'

Give a clarion call.
Open your heart,
open your mind,
unlock all manmade gates,
let it be all open;
open for you, open for him,
open for me, open for one,
and open for all .

Your children would be then saved
from modern school prisons,
and would taste what is humane,
what is true civilization.
Open nature
is the best way
to get human face institution.

91. Let River Dry

If a river goes
in between you and me,
if neither you nor me
Know how to swim,
Should we then wait
waving hands
from either bank
and cry, Hi!
Instead of learning
how to swim
Should we pray, 'Let the river dry'.

92. Woman No Longer

I am a woman
I am now not known by lips,
or, by brow plucked eyes,
nor, by my balls,
nor, by hairs falls,
nor, by polished nails at all,
nor, by my husky inviting voice,
nor, by my pose and poise.

You can't compare me with flowers,
nor, with gentle hilly rivers,
nor, with dew drops on grass blades,
nor, with silver and gold cascades.
I am now a 'PERSON'
I am now a bunch of human ambitions.

I am now a stronger sex.

Forget to call me, 'my fair lady'.
I am now a to z human comedy
and tragedy intertwined.
What I am I determine.
Man, if you are thunder clouds
I am million Volt lightning.
Who are you to be sorry for my plight?

I am ever proud for me
as my all aspects are ever beautiful and bright.

93. Lies

If you implore a river to flow upstream
she would do.
If you ask the mountain to move
He, 'cause of love, would do.
Ask your lover not to tell lies
She would freshly invent
and with a deep sigh
would say, 'You brute,
Lies are sweeter than truth.'

'I love you, I love you, I love you'
Fill the air and the sky.
Do you say, all these are TRUTH,
aren't they 'LIE'?

94. Literature A Game Of Words

Literature is a game of words.
With new and new word power
techniques of disclosures are easier,
exposition is clearer,
versions are smoother.
Poems and prose
on word strength they enforce,
on words they survive
through ages and lives.

It is anybody
who can coin new terms and words.
daily railways commuters are the best discoverers,
(as I found in India)
public bus conductors too in the third world
make novel uses by their wit and sense of humor

Dictionaries are fattening by the demand of customers.
Incorporate the new words
and terms with illustration
to increase writing power.

Poets are servants,
words are master.

95. Lovely

Lovely are those who act lovely,
positive throughout.
Smilingly they accept defeat.
Calmly they divide loss or profit.
Labyrinth, however, their path may appear
they make it straighter.
With perseverance and patience
they go easily up the ladder.
Modesty and forbearance is their treasure.

Material world they need just for existence,
soul satisfying livelihood is their intention.

Nothing they preserve except goodness in character,
everything they throw away if it is humanity spoiler.
Kind words they scatter.
Peace they preserve
love they deserve.
Covetousness they reserve.

96. Years Left To Live

Years yet to live through
be like that,
I live with mind free,
head up in pride of honesty,
tongue tells the truth,
eyes see beauty,
and ears listen to messages of the Almighty.
Let my hands work for who cannot work,
let my legs reach the destitute sharp,
my back carries the infirm,
and I can rub the pain balm
to those who are faultless but harmed.

Oh, my master!
these small prayers of mine
be fully granted in fine.
I know I have not many miles to go.
All human beings suffer from limitations.
By them many things are seen
but many, many things remain unseen.

97. Corruption

Man will come,
man will go.
Manhood stays.
Society stays,
stays with it many facets.
Politics is the everlasting accomplice.
Corruption is sweet progeny of political prowess.
Who is to blame?
Genes in man!
Society, system, environment!
All play combined actions.

Who will be the mightiest corrector,
the gene manipulators?

Greed and jealousy genes operate together.
Corruption is something
that the rich and the poor share.
I am not a pessimist.
Yet that corruption will vanish someday
I will never declare.
It can reduce to a significant extent
if there is sincere and honest political commitments.

98. Bird Peon

In days of great Sanskrit poet, KALIDAS
Birds used to carry love letters
from princesses to princes or kings.
And Clouds too fluttered wings
in love letters carrying.

Today as I watch below
in my lane
Girls and boys hold mobile phones,
press hard on ears,
speak to each other.
They are incessant heart's message tellers

Vanished have written letters.
I called Kalidas;
'What about writing love poems now'.
He said,'I can take a vow
if I were born in your days
and blessed with a mobile phone
I would have freed all peon birds from my cage,
allowed them to eat from my book page after page.

Wiser are mobile phones,
Ears and lips overwork.
Thanks to electronics when deluge cuts
Lovers, unperturbed, never fail to chat.'

99. Chairs Interchange

Today you are in heaven,
I am in hell.
Tomorrow I am in heaven;
you are in hell;
'cause both of us are hand in hand
in the same surface trails.

All powerful politics decides,
who will drink from whose bottle
and eat from whose plate.
Dish they serve as they wish
in their own rates.

Heaven's chair is in their hands,
Hell's throne too;
interchange they at their convenience

as they know the clue.
I know not I can get a chair
By befitting payments,
or, by most humble prayers.

100. Flute Player

In my inner most hut
There lives a flute player
Who took shelter there
when I was a boy mere.

Often when I am ready to sleep
He would ask me to remain awake
He would play the flute
The silence of nature would with joy break.
His music will over flow the meadow,
shake the leaves in the nearby forest,
his music would create ripples in lakes,
and would make dance the venomous snakes.
Many times I sit spell bound
forgetting my night meals to eat
How I confess and admit over years
He has captured me bit by bit.
Who is that flute player
If I try to draw his profile
He does not stand in my front,
would move away with a mystery smile.
That day when, on appeal and prayer,
He showed his part face by removing the veil,
to my utter wonder I deciphered
It is my favorite poet and singer

Tagore, ever young in heart and soul.
He would never cease to play flute
Calling his RADHA, my INNER ME,
Whose heart he long back stole
with a cupid wand of poetic beauty.

101. Rating

I rated a rivulet as a river,
a river as a sea,
a sea as an ocean;
How I would rate your tears
when you bid me last farewell bye
I don't know.

Now I am at a mountain top,
you float in a boat in a lake.
Your lakes liken your eyes.
My mountain shrinks as a mole hill.
ALAS! I forgot the taste of the last kiss.

You are the rivulet.
You are the river, sea, ocean all the same.
My mountain is a mole hill.
There is none to blame.
Why forgetting you
since your last kiss and hug
I am not yet put to shame.

102. Innocent Susan

I met Susan Brem in India when I was 35 and she 30'
her husband Fred 40.
They were nice persons ever I have seen.
They were Americans.
I spoke to them, liked and loved.
After three years I was taken by Susan
to Lincoln's memorial
at Wash. DC.
Has not changed she.
At dinner at her house her husband was found struck with
melancholy.
What had happened? I questioned.
He said 'most photographs taken in India were taken away
by pilferers'.
She then showed a movie of a bullock cart loaded with paddy;
two skin and bone bullocks
were pulling at their best under constant whip.
Husband and wife exclaimed, ' BEAUTIFUL!'
I cried, 'why!'
They were silenced by my impolite shouting.
The thief had stolen this wonderful India.
I silently uttered 'thank you, MR thief.'
I said, sorry,
took my bag and bid 'good night'.
I had never met them thereafter.
I love India, I love USA too.
God knows, when my country
would get rid of BULLOCK CART POVERTY.

103. Give Me More Words, My Lord!

Words mean in life
None else,
Words are friend, philosopher and guide,
Words are base.
The day you make me
See your light on earth
It is sounds and words
That was of all worth.

104. Roof Top Gardener

Whosoever far and near,
Come to my garden upstairs.
There the chrysanthemums sing,
Marigolds dance in wind,
Dahlias enjoy vibrant fun,
Roses are fragrance jocund,
The blue and the white Aparajitas
are shy, and love the sun.

My friends,
everyday early morning
I caress them as my girls,
Kiss them, hug and pat them
as my own pals.

They would bid me goodbye in a few days.
They promise to come every year,
'come what may'

105. To My Son

(when he was striving for medial post graduation in USA)

Top of the hill
is at the top,
the bottom
at the bottom.

You are in between.

You can move up to the top,
you can go down to the bottom of the hill.
Both require strength and skill.

You have two options,
my dear son.
Do as you like.
None would challenge your decision.
You can enjoy the top with other toppers.
From the top, indeed,
the valley beneath is greener,
the sky above is sparklingly bluer.

106. Come In

Come in, come in my old friend,
friendship is old but you are never.
Do you wear the smile as you had been,
do you have the same majesty as you walk,
do you have the same wit as you talk?

Man does not change.
Genes do not permit.
Environment casts a spell.
Still as you are, I greet.

When you revisit me
with the advent of the next spring
dahlia s would dance,
and marigold would sing
I will study your fingers as before
and slip a silver ring.

I am no more a king.

107. Poems' Resort

Poems, I live with.
Poems, I love.
Poems often fly to heaven
like a grey dove.
I kiss them on cheeks,
Kiss them on lips,
I keep them on bosom,
I don't let them slip.
Out of sight when they are
I send an
ardent prayer:
'Come back, come back soon'.
And I promise,
I would not let your hands go,
Give you my all fortune.

108. Hush Genes

Hush genes work in every soul.
Souls bear with when hushed.
Life moves on wheels of
hushing and being hushed.

Could you name a Celeb
Who was never hushed,
or, who had not hushed?

In some moments
These genes are switched off.
But the hushing process does not flop.
In civilization
Hush genes are never ever mutated to perish.
Only a mutant variety does often flourish.

109. When I Peep Into

When I peeped into your world
where you are the king, the queen and the attendant,
where you read to yourself, mock and jeer
where you preserve and scatter as you wish
I am amused, my master.

Multi dimensional world
goes on adding dimensions,
even black lead pencil sketches
look rain bow perfection.
My inner personal world has no boundaries,
has no horizon,
limitless is its extension.

Guests, or, no guests
there go on party dances and songs.
Many events are transient,
many events are prolonged.

My peeping into your world,
setting aside mine,
me thought, you saw my protruding nose,
and would call me
with you to dine.

110. Cool Nest To Rest

When I was in a watching tower in HENRY Island
at about the sun set,
to my wonder I saw,
the smart red shirt wearing Sun
was trying to find his retiring bed
dipping in a small pond
amidst a lash, green verge,
denying the covetable call of the deep sea close by.
The whole day's hard labor requires a peaceful nest
to rest.
The cool pond's inviting eyes
had no vice.
The Sun was wise
His huge prestige
of dipping into the sea to compromise.

Back home,
should I not try for a nest,
should I not rest on those virgin breasts,
should I not sing to young ears
folk love lines collected over years
from my cowboy rural friend
who sang, while grazing meek lambs all alone?
Those days of mine are no more.
What is the harm if I reminisce,
if I dream.

At dawn when the Sun will get up fresh and gay
I will pray,
'Don't leave the pond rest
for vanity and pride call of the sea.
If you leave at all,
give to me'.

III. The Factory Gate Drama

The factory gate was closed,
one worker died in harness.
Widow with her three teenagers
prayed for compensation.
The manager denied the demise.
Where is then my husband otherwise?
There was confrontation.
The manager said, 'one casual labor died'.
'Was he my man', the woman cried.
'No, he was my husband', cried another
brought to the scene by the rival T.U. leader.
For claims and counter claims
by two wives with six children,
names of women age etc. were the same,
so for the children.
This made the manager happy.
Trade union leaders of different affiliations
stood differently for wives.

All on a sudden one wife, a little younger,
shouted against a T. U. leader,
'You dragged me here.
I was quite happy with my profession,
though ashamed now of my confession'.

'I will go, let the gate open.
You all go for your work
I would go for mine'.
The manager was amused,
the circus was over.
T.U. leaders looked at each other's face.
There is no need of dragging the case.

Wonder of wonders!
First woman also fled
when the dead worker appeared,
beaten and profusely bled.
No one was wife.
No one was dead.
The rumor had spread.

112. When I Will Depart

When I will depart
who cares,
I am securely tied or not
to the cot
that will take me to the Burning Ghat[*],
who cares,
who weep or cry,
who cares,
who meet in condolence,
who prayed, what was prayed in admiration.

But I would care
That my poems and all writings
go into safe custodian hands.

My writings are my speaking contributions.
They would say,
'he came, he conceived, he created.
Out of love,
he allowed everything to float
for us to view
on eternal drops of dew'.

---

[*] **Burning Ghat:** The cemetery where the dead bodies of the HINDU are burnt to ashes.

I repeat my prayer here:

'place some of my books
on my dead bosom'.
Floral wreaths are costly.
Books will better decorate
more placidly, in lieu.

113. I Shall Carry On

My age says,
'look at the setting sun'.
My mind refuses,
and says,
'I am already refueled full tank'
A love of 23
has reached my bank.
She would give me
a share of her dividends.

My heart is not shy to declare,
'you are still a beginner.
Your evening will show
nights and following days together.
You would lead from the front.
There is no wonder'.

Allow me to comment:
Free from age linked impositions,
to the best of my god gifted ability
I shall carry on and on
Without breaks,
With soulful purpose and intention

Hiding face behind two unfolded palms
life smiles.
Death showing his back to my door
Says to his partner, life,
'though I don't agree fully,
But I can take rest for a god while.'

114. Lulls To Sleep

I am a child of 70.
My mother left for her heavenly abode
about thirty Years before.
I still covet,
My mother to sing for me
Lulling song
To cover like a warming cover
for a soothing slumber.
My mother,
I think,
does not live so distanced from me.
She hears my prayer.
For her songs
I, a pampered child'
Have so keen ears
that I clearly hear:
She sings my favorite lulling lines.
I sleep deep,
as if, on her breast sublime.

115. Sea View Or Pin Head

When I am only mine
I lose the luster and shine.
When I divide
Amongst many
Gone is ego-agony,
I am again smooth and fine.

When my all is for you
I am just a wide sea view,
the limitless blue.

Outside the self
Dances the nature,
Inside selfishness murmurs.
Avarice- mountains and hills,
Despite their heights,
Cannot block the sun,
cannot debar bird's flight.

There are no bars,
there are no barriers,
For an inquisitive mind
that likes to go on for probes deeper.

When you muse and search your soul,
The soul says,' why in me alone',
out go far and farther.
I am scattered all over'.

Keeping aloof from the world
You are just a pin head.
Spreading liberal into nature
Your one half is a great receiver,
the other half is an equal giver.

Sharing in the surroundings your treasure
You are just like a gleefully flowing river.

Aloof in your heart's corner
You are just a bowl of water.
In no time you vaporize away,
left dry and dead,
like the destiny of a water drop
of the size of a pin head.

116. Two Wheeler

Love is other name of sacrifice,
lust is utterly selfish.
When lust guides love
it is a total finish;
Neither lust is fully enjoyable,
nor is love at all accomplished.

Love may guide lust.
If it is bidirectional
from you to me,
and me to you,
Life is a divine bliss.

Lust is also not merely physical,
nor is love only mental.
One is partner of other.
Love - Lust is a two wheeler
to propagate through the course eternal.

I am for both,
but more for love.
I am for life
without extreme curb.

117. Flame Of Love

Dawn never broke,
clouds never did shift veil,
sunshine was ever a dream,
it was not dark even.

You were just a few yards away.
I knew from fragrance.
But neither I could see
nor could I touch.
My love, art thou an illusion!

This was/ is my life.
I do not blame.
I am got to live
without peace and fame.
There burns a flame
heating and consuming,
would it burn me to ash
before you I can encash?

Love, where art thou!
Save me from a deluge flash.
If I am so washed down
I may, on stone guard, get crashed.

118. Bleed And Plead

Incognito when i bleed
there is none beside to treat
only a girl of eighteen does plead
your agony i can read
you are betrayed; god forbid,
they will similarly bleed
not incognito
but in open field,
and there will be none
for them to plead.

The girl said, "I am from heaven
and in no time you will accompany me
to your coveted destination.
As long as i am there with you
you should not have hesitation".

I bled and died.
To that nobody took pity,
nobody cried.
Many said
"his death was justified".

119. Loneliness

Loneliness engulfed me.
Had it been in a resort
I could have conquered
with some picturesque nature
around my hut.
But in a town life
it redoubles its paralyzing power
I spend time day dreaming
with things that visit me haphazard.

Loneliness has often poetic character,
but when prolonged
it tells up on the heart
and instead of lowering
it goes on boosting cardiac pressure.
When I was active in service
loneliness I preferred
in retired life
it seems to be a slow killer.
Loneliness, forgive me;
I will not keep your company any further.

120. None And Nothing To Fear

My love,
the sky is yours,
the earth is yours,
you have none and nothing to fear.
To mother- nature you are so dear.

If your vision is clear,
forget all confounding factors.
Move on the force of love
Me, your closest to the heart
would always be there.

My love,
Everybody seeks love,
not only children and parents,
not only dating pairs,
all around everything
raises the solemn prayer,
"love be there, love be there".

The sky is yours,
'Cause, love is yours,
the earth too is yours as love is yours.

Between the sky and the earth
mother nature spreads herself
in love and only in love.

Why would you then fear!
I know your vision is crystal clear.
We can easily sort out confounding factors.

121. Hook Or Crook

Politicians love only to be in power
by hook or by crook.
They know no enemy.
They would hold hands of me
though I am dead against,
if only they find
I am of that kind,
that is, I am either a hook
or, for them a crook.

I will ensure to book
the power and the chair;
it is their only prayer.

Politics is a game
that does not discriminate
between the foul play and the rules.

Every thing is pure and pious
if it suits the purpose
of power politics,
of chair politics.

and any slogan is enough good
if it helps to keep the leader charismatic.

Let hooks work well,
let crooks work fine.
The politicians would then feel sublime.

122. Reunion

When reunion will come off
with my only soul mate,
with my man in my heart,
in whose soul
I am and only me live apart..

Through thousands of years
I have been getting birth after birth,
and death after death,
but where is he?
Is he in my breath!

Human life is a baffling query.
Soul searching I found
that I should not wait weary
My mate shall meet me must
after finishing his round.

If you do not know who he is
and how he looks like,
that means he is mixed up
in everything in your left and right.

It is the knowledge,
it is the consciousness,
it is soul searching ability,
by which you can understand,
in every transient birth to death,
you were part of eternity.
Separate reunion therefore
was not at all a necessity.

123. Do Not Stay Away

Can a poet stay away from current affairs
Societal, political, religious and economics?
No, he/she cannot.
Their pens or computer screens
again and again will flash
about all sorts of human concerns and clash.

When I am agonized on incidence of any kind
my soul cries to give a vent
of my feelings.
When it is a political assault on personal right
I get fright inside,
if the ruffians take revenge on pleas
for my anguish.
For a moment I shrink.
Then forsaking the fear
I like to tear
open the demon design.
As a poet
then I feel, I am doing fine.

124. Cover Page

Those who go by cover page
And indulge in window shopping,
Those who hardly go into the pages and lines,
Those who are enticed by appearance,
How would they taste the heart's content
How would they appreciate mental relation!

When I got her
The cover was demolished.
Preface and introduction were abolished.
She stood naked as fact of life.
Searching within
I took her as my wife.
Anything she had not disguised
Life is moving with ease.
I would vehemently ascertain,
for descent relation,
the cover page is unimportant.

Give any vibrant cover
when you two
have thoroughly known each other.
Life is like a book.
See the cover page,
but don't stop there.

Into some inner pages you get.
Then decide whether you select or reject.

125. Shield Of Lies

Lies are there.
Lies are here,
Lies are/were everywhere.

Lies are in heaven,
on which gods ever depend
to keep the throne,
as and when the demons do threaten.

Lies are intelligent creation.
If lies are gone, truths do not stand.
Against the canvass of sweet lies
lives appear so vibrant.

Lovers' lies are innocent.

Such lies do not harm but charm,
they protect, save and sooth,
they please and heal to move smooth.
Consoling lies are far better
than the pinching hard truths.

Lovers stand on lies,
so wives and husbands.
Because of lies only
the wheels of life are so resonant.

Let us live up to and with sweetest lies
to cover up undue human anguish.
Mind, you, my beautiful dating miss,
Your every day lies are ever sweeter
than your anger loaded kiss.

126. A Cup Of Green Tea

A cup of green tea
In the early morning with a news daily
Is a heaven on earth for me.
In fact, the whole night even in sleep
I dream of a slightly rosy beauty
As a sixteen damsel, my green tea.

Often I go to my friend Dhiranjoy,
I asked him, 'Above 60, how your is sex'.
He says, 'Fine'. And I ask, 'How come'
He says aloud,
'Just a few cups of green tea
Keep me young for sex, believe me'.

Another day
I met a novelist and story writer above 80.
He is busy compiling his 6th volume.
I trespassed and asked,
How you do this compilation,
It requires energy and patience.'
He said with his usual eloquence,
'I started green tea
When I was touching sixty,
At plus eighty
I left not her (green tea, as if her love) company.
So 'am free of agony'.

As I was walking down a book shop lane
some known woman voice
Did call me from past golden.
She was a 60 plus class mate
Standing with her 70 plus husband.
I wondered
After a gap of forty years
How could she
Recognized me!
She said, 'Easy, you are
As you were before'.
I said, 'You were never my admirer.
'Now I am', said lightly she.
You have become slightly oldish.
How it could be'?
I said, 'Perhaps, it is green tea.
Green tea keeps you green
And make sweetly grin'.

I got so a lover of 60
Looking like a 16
Both of us take tea green.

127. Absent Minded

Nature is absent minded,
And is unusual forgetful,
And as she commits
She is also a great forgiver,
And so much relinquisher
That she easily eases herself
Without a pain killer.
Leaving me amidst storms and dry leaves
She went out with her recent lover,
Catarina, a naughty girl,
To make a business agreement
On disaster surfaced goods to share.
I wonder
Whether I should wait for her,
Or, take a new and fresh partner.

She is forgetful and absent minded
though not suffering from Alzheimer.

On the road to this point
How many times I kissed her
She was forgetful of that smarter.

She had promised me a gift of the spring
With all its colorful, fragrant flowers.
Now I find that she is busy
For me to build a severe winter

An absent minded as she is
She is also a forgetful ever.

Last time when she left me,
Went out accompanying a typhoon boy
Leaving behind her shadowing umbrella
Like an old aged human visitor.

128. By Definition

Darkness defines light.
The good unveils the bad.
Bravery can easily shun cowardice.
Virtue is hard to separate from vice.
Man and woman are complimentary,
Wonderfully the society comprises of them.
Devils constantly develop a separate group,
living here with much hue and cry.
Civilized people live silent and shy.
Gentlemen are not so blessed,
they are, by definition, 'small fry'.

129. Receding Horizon

In my front dancing sea waves
Enter through a grilled window.
They came from the eastern horizon
Uninvited to tease my morning vision.
'Where from'? as I asked, they said, 'Lo, there',
Pointing to the horizon, their mother.
'What is there stored for me?' when
I asked, they said, 'Seeing is believing,
The beauty is hardly describable in words.
There my mother is calm and quiet, golden and blue
Yellow and rosy, saffron and all hues.
There the birds do really sing,
The bees do not sting.
Rather they all day offer honey's spring,
There the mountains speak, the fountains flight
All do everything with sweetness of sunset light'.

I shrank.
for, here I am soiled and viled.
Would they accept me even for a moment while!
They assured, 'As we go back
Ride on us safe
We shall take you there
With out a break.

Doubted I started,
Went miles and miles and miles
But was unable to view mother's smiles
As I was told.
When I started to scold they said, 'How can you see
You are yet to reach the horizon'.
True so, I forget that out of excitement.

As I said, 'When could we reach?'
They said, 'When you see the greenish beach'.
More they took me inside
More I got frustrated.
To that they said, 'You must be a sinner,
That is why more we go to the close
More the horizon receded far.

130. Share To Be Shared

Share to be shared.
Share my pain;
I shall allow you
to share my pleasure.
I shall share your suffering
you share my tearing.
Every turn of life need share.
The glare of destiny
does not spare.
Share with me all while
when I have indulged in war
against the social tormentors.
Sharing is caring,
Sharing is just becoming a brother
Who shared mother's breast,
Who got father's love and care.
Together
we share the Sun light,
we share the sky,
we share the breeze and air.
When Nature inflicted TSunami
We together suffered.
Why can't we now
share the blows in fight
against social tormentors!